AF374793

The Author
Of The Book
I Didn't Get To
Write

Samone' Cross

Dedication

To every woman who has ever had to rebuild herself from pieces she never asked to hold—

This is for you.

To my children, who gave me reasons to rise on days when I didn't know how—you are my heartbeat, my why, my greatest becoming.

To the version of me who survived storms, people will never fully understand—I honor you. You walked through fire so that I could stand here today, whole and rising.

To anyone who has ever felt abandoned, unseen, or unworthy—may these pages remind you that healing is possible, that strength can be quiet, and that becoming is a journey, not a destination.

This book is for the fighters, the dreamers, the overcomers, the daughters who refuse to stay bound through life's difficult challenges—keep moving to the flow of the true Author's pen. God is still writing your story.

This book is for us.

Samone' (Sa-mo-nay)

Table of Contents

Chapter 1:
The Good Days-So I Thought

Psalm 34:18 (NIV)
"The Lord is close to the brokenhearted and saves those
who are crushed in spirit."

Before everything changed, there were good days, and there were days the kind that smelled like dust and sunscreen and sounded like laughter echoing off the bleachers. My mom kept me busy with rec softball and cheering. That was our thing, our way of bonding. She loved softball, and I think that's where I got my love for it, too. She'd be on the sidelines, shouting plays and cheering louder than anyone else, with my little sister sitting beside her, waving her tiny pom-poms like she was part of the team.

Those were the moments that made me feel seen, the moments where it was just us. The late-night rides home after games with the windows down and the air thick with the smell of dirt and victory. Her smile. Her pride. For a while, that was enough to make me believe we were unbreakable.

But one day, something took a turn.

My mother got married when I was ten. I had a baby sister, who was five years younger than me, and when my mom married, I gained another sister, six years younger. Life started to feel different after that. The attention that used to be mine now had to be shared, and I didn't quite know where I fit anymore. There was love in the house, but it felt crowded, like there wasn't enough space for me and all my feelings.

At 12, my mom sent me to live with my grandma — no explanation, no conversation, no choice. One day I was home, the next I was packing my life into bags I didn't understand I'd be carrying for years. I remember the silence more than anything, the way it said everything she couldn't, or wouldn't. I tried to make sense of it, to believe it was temporary, but deep down I knew something had shifted. That moment planted a question in me that would follow me into womanhood: *What did I do to make love leave?*

Living with my grandma meant being sheltered and protected in some ways, but confined in others. I couldn't go anywhere, couldn't hang out with friends, couldn't do much of anything unless it involved going to stay with my grandma on my dad's side. The house felt like both a safe haven and a cage. She meant well, I know that now that her strictness was her way of keeping me safe in a world she knew could be cruel. But back then, it felt like I was being punished for something no one ever named.

For a while, I found comfort in spending time with my dad. Those visits gave me a glimpse of freedom, of belonging. I could laugh a little louder, talk a little freer. For a moment, I could pretend that maybe I wasn't so easily forgotten. But that changed once he got married. Suddenly, that door closed too. The weekends I was supposed to spend with him turned into weekends at his mother's house instead. He would drop me off and leave, and I'd spend those days wondering why everyone kept sending me away.

It felt like being loved from a distance was always close enough to see, but never close enough to touch. I'd watch him drive away, his truck disappearing down the road, and I'd whisper to myself, *Maybe next time he'll stay.* But next time always came the same way the last one ended, with me waiting.

I learned early that waiting could feel like a full-time job. Waiting to be chosen. Waiting to be wanted. Waiting for someone to notice the quiet ache sitting behind my smile. I became good at pretending, pretending I was okay, pretending I understood, and pretending it didn't hurt. But inside, I was unraveling in small, silent ways.

My grandma's house became the backdrop of my growth, the place where I discovered how to keep my feelings folded neatly in the corners of my heart. There were nights I'd lie awake, listening to the hum of the old refrigerator and the ticking clock on the wall, wondering if my mom ever thought about me before she fell asleep. I'd imagine her voice, her laugh, the sound of her keys at the door, and all the ordinary things that used to make me feel safe.

Sometimes, I'd picture myself walking back into her house and her telling me it was all a mistake, that she missed me, that she needed me, that she was sorry. But that day never came. Instead, I grew up learning how to live without explanations.

And maybe that's where my strength started, not in being fearless, but in learning how to keep standing when the people I loved kept walking away. Because the truth is, when love leaves without warning, you learn to create your own kind of home inside yourself, the one that doesn't disappear when someone else does.

From the outside, I was just a small-town girl trying to find my place in a world that didn't seem to have a place for me. I was the one who smiled through the pain, who hid bruises not on my skin but on my spirit. The one who was bullied for being different, too loud, too ambitious, too "extra," they said. But what they didn't know was that I had a grandmother who refused to let me fade into the background.

Grandma believed in keeping me busy, keeping me visible, keeping me thriving. If I wasn't at church ushering or singing in the youth choir, I was somewhere representing the local NAACP chapter, walking across stages in fashion shows, or cheering my heart out at rec games. I played softball, I danced, I smiled, I performed, and even when I didn't feel like it, Grandma made sure I showed up. She used to say, *"You never know who's watching. Always give them something good to see."*

And so, I discovered to perform not just on stages, but in life. To keep my head high, even when my heart was heavy. To clap for others even when it felt like no one was clapping for me. But what happens when the world sees too much, and not enough, all at once?

At fourteen, my life took a turn I wasn't prepared for. I became a mom before I even figured out who I was. The same mouths that used to tease me now whispered louder: *"She'll be nothing."* Teachers looked at me with pity. Friends drifted away, and adults smiled with that kind of sympathy that stings more than it soothes. I could almost feel the labels wrapping around me: fast girl, lost girl, statistic.

But inside, something else was growing. A spark. A fight. A whisper that said, *"You'll see."*

As I got older, that whisper turned into a hunger. I wanted to be seen again, but this time on my own terms. I wanted to rewrite the story everyone thought they already knew about me. I turned to the industry for the lights, the cameras, and the attention. It was a world that promised validation, even if it came wrapped in temptation. I posed for men's magazines, smiled for flashing lights, and showed up in music videos. People called me a *video vixen,* but really, I was a girl trying to feel powerful in a world that once made her feel invisible.

And maybe that's the thing about pain, it doesn't always break you down. Sometimes, it builds you into someone who refuses to be unseen.

Chapter 2:
Before It All Changed

Proverbs 16:9 (NIV)
"In their hearts humans plan their course, but the Lord
establishes their steps."

Before the chaos, before the betrayal, before the moment everything shattered, there was me.

I had developed an instinct that showed me how to survive, how to stand tall, how to keep moving even when my heart felt overwhelmed. But surviving didn't mean I was okay. I carried the weight of years, of choices I didn't fully understand, and of doors that had been closed before I could even knock. Still, I was restless. After years of being boxed in, judged, and dismissed, I craved something bigger, something that made me feel alive, something that reminded me I still had a place in the world.

But survival didn't mean sainthood.

There was a time when the night called louder than God ever did. The music, the lights, the freedom that occurred after years of being overlooked, I drank it up like oxygen. I was in the clubs, in music videos, in VIP sections. I brushed shoulders with rappers, ballplayers, and street legends who smelled like danger and designer cologne. They saw me. They spoiled me. They made me feel alive in ways I hadn't known were possible.

Even at my wildest, though, there was always a voice deep down, calling me back to purpose. A voice that sounded a lot like my grandmother's. The same grandmother who raised me on church pews and protest marches, who dressed me up for talent shows and taught me to speak from both the diaphragm and the heart.

I was never meant to be average. But when you're trying to outrun pain, average can start to feel like peace.

Still, something was shifting. In the quiet moments, after the parties, after the road trips, and after the staged smiles, I could feel it in my gut: a storm was coming. I didn't know when or how, but I knew life as I knew it wasn't going to stay the same.

And I was right.

Because everything I thought I knew and everything I thought was real was about to unravel.

I spent my early twenties chasing attention, chasing validation, chasing power in the places I thought I could find it. I posed for magazines, appeared in music videos, smiled for flashing lights, and rubbed shoulders with people who made the world feel bigger than the one I had grown up in. I wanted to be seen again, but this time, on my terms.

And for a while, it worked. I felt untouchable, magnetic, alive. But the higher you climb chasing someone else's definition of success, the further you get from yourself. I thought I was winning, but really, I was losing a part of me along the way, and the parts that knew love without conditions, the parts that trusted without hesitation, the parts that hadn't yet hardened against the world.

I was discovering that validation is temporary, that applause doesn't fill the emptiness, and that freedom without roots can feel more like drifting than living. But even in the chaos, even in the flashing lights and the late nights, a small part of me was always listening to that quiet voice, that tether pulling me back to purpose.

It took me years to understand that the power I'd been chasing wasn't out there, it was in me all along. But before I could reach it, I had to lose myself first.

And that's exactly what happened next.

Chapter 3:
In the Middle of It

Isaiah 41:10 (NIV)
"So do not fear, for I am with you; do not be dismayed, for
I am your God. I will strengthen you and help you; I will
uphold you with my righteous right hand."

By the time I hit my early twenties, I had become *that* girl. The one people whispered about when they walked into a room. Known. Visible. Magnetic. My presence didn't just fill spaces; it shifted them. I could turn a quiet night into a story people would tell for weeks. I knew the DJs, the promoters, the ballplayers. I met people who made the city pulse and the ones who controlled the nights that felt endless and alive. My confidence lingered like perfume long after I left.

But in a city driven by ego, status, and secrets, being popular wasn't always a blessing.

In that world, it was never really about *who you were,* but it was about *who you were connected to.* And I had connections. The kind that opened velvet ropes, put my name on flyers, and landed me in VIP sections most people only saw through a screen. But those same connections also brought envy, gossip, and snakes dressed in stilettos.

I started running with a crew of other "city girls," the group that had beautiful, fearless, always put-together girls. Each of them had her own claim to fame: the body, the boyfriend, the clout, the story. Together, we were a scene, a vibe, a headline. On the surface, it looked like sisterhood, powerful women chasing dreams and living life out loud. But underneath the glitz was something fragile, unspoken, and ready to explode.

I chased every night like it was my last. I posed for magazine spreads, smiled through music video shoots, and laughed at jokes I didn't find funny just to be in the circle. I drove through streets lined with neon lights, feeling untouchable. I danced in clubs where the bass rattled your bones and the air smelled of perfume, alcohol, and ambition. I drank it in like oxygen. Finally, I felt seen.

But even in all of it, a small voice inside me, the one that sounded a lot like my grandmother's, whispered, *"Baby, don't forget who you are."* I tried to push it aside. I wanted the freedom. I wanted the attention. I wanted to feel like the girl who had once been invisible mattered. But that feeling stayed like a shadow, and I couldn't shake it, reminding me I wasn't just chasing fun. I was chasing something I hadn't yet named.

My great-grandmother had always told me, *"When people show you who they are, believe them. And sometimes, you just gotta leave them where they at."*

Back then, I wasn't ready to leave anyone behind. I wasn't paying attention to the signs. I was living the moment, and the moment felt intoxicating.

There were late-night studio sessions, weekends that blurred into mornings, and conversations full of hidden agendas. I rubbed shoulders with names that turned heads and laughed in places where secrets hid in plain sight. I convinced myself I had found my tribe and a circle of women who understood the grind, the glitter, and the hustle. I wanted to believe we had each other's backs.

But trust is fragile in a world built on image, and cracks always show eventually.

The breaking point came wrapped in betrayal.

Noelle, known in the Tri-Cities as "Ell," was the oldest in our group, the one everyone respected. She had presence, power, and a way of commanding attention without saying a word. But when I found out she had started seeing someone from my past, a man I once kicked it with, fresh out and sitting on a little money, the air shifted.

It wasn't just about a man. It was about loyalty. Code. Respect. And once that line was crossed, the sisterhood fractured silently.

We tried to hold it together and had forced brunches, staged laughter in crowded lounges, pretending nothing had shifted. But deep down, we all knew the truth. Something sacred between us had died quietly.

I remember one night driving home from a club, city lights bouncing off the windshield, the kind of night that feels alive in your chest but hollow in your soul. Noelle broke the silence.

"What are you gonna do if modeling doesn't work out for you?"

Her voice was casual, but the weight behind it hit me. I didn't flinch. I didn't even look at her.

"I sell houses," I said.

Calm. Certain. Like I was speaking my future into existence.

That was the last night we hung out.

No drama. No tears. No argument. Just distance. I didn't call. I didn't chase. I didn't question. I let it go. Somewhere deep down, I understood that sometimes God removes people before they ruin what He's building.

Within a year, I enrolled in real estate school. I studied hard, learned every rule, every process, every deal. And just like I said, I became an agent.

Because no matter what the world took from me, faith, friends, love, one thing about me:

I always kept my word.

Chapter 4:
Finding My Way Through

Psalm 32:8 (NIV)
"I will instruct you and teach you in the way you should
go; I will counsel you with my loving eye on you."

Getting my real estate license was supposed to be *my* breakthrough. My fresh start. The "new me" that the old me had always dreamed of becoming. I imagined myself walking into open houses, closing deals, and building a life on my own terms. But the truth is, healing doesn't happen in a straight line. Sometimes, even when I said I was done, I still craved the chaos I was trying to escape.

Even after I stepped into my new career, the "fun girl" in me wasn't completely gone. She was just quiet for a while, waiting in the wings. Every now and then, she'd show up heels on, ready to hit the city, ready for the lights, the attention, the thrill. And if I'm being honest, there was something about those industry men I couldn't quite let go of— the charm, the lifestyle, the trips, and the fine dining. They knew how to entertain, and I loved being entertained.

For a while, it was intoxicating. I felt alive in ways that real estate couldn't give me. I was the girl who could close a deal in the morning and be at a rooftop party by nightfall, laughing as if nothing else mattered. But eventually, the glitter started to dull. The late nights no longer felt exciting; they started to feel heavy.

Somewhere between open houses and late-night linkups, I met *him*.

He was well-known in the industry—a dope boy with connections, a face people respected or feared—depending on who you asked. People were shocked when they found out we were together. *"When did that happen?" "Why him?" "How did Mone' end up with him?"* What they didn't see was that we'd been lowkey for a while with quiet trips, hidden dates, and inside jokes only we shared.

I thought I had found someone who understood both sides of me: the boss and the wild child.

But settling down with him wasn't settling at all; it was suffocating.

At first, it was intoxicating. Spontaneous getaways. Hotel suites with skyline views. Dinners that ended with room service and rose petals. He knew how to sweep a girl off her feet, and for a moment, I let myself believe in the fantasy. But as soon as the thrill wore off, his true colors started to bleed through. Compliments turned into criticism. Protection turned into control.

He never had to raise a hand; his words cut deep enough.

He isolated me slowly, cleverly. Every time I tried to pull away, he'd plan another escape. Another trip. Another distraction. He knew I loved a good time, and he weaponized it against me. The cycle was predictable: fight, distance, getaway, rewind. And I let it happen because part of me still wanted to believe in the fantasy.

But the mask was slipping. While I sat in the house, losing pieces of myself, he was out living single, entertaining his baby mama, flirting with anyone who smiled too long. The disrespect was bold; the lies were even bolder. And every time I tried to leave, he'd show up with calls, texts, driving past my mama's house at night, acting like *I* was the problem.

They say people accuse you of what they're doing, and he was a textbook example of that.

I started staying at my mom's, or my grandmother's, just to breathe, just to remind myself I existed outside of him. And when I needed a deeper kind of peace, I'd spend time with my dad's mom—my other grandmother, the pastor. She kept me rooted, grounded. Just like when I was younger, she'd make sure I was active in church, whether I wanted to sing, usher, or help out somewhere. Being around her reminded me of who I was beneath it all.

But peace never lasted long.

One night, I made a decision that I wasn't going to sit at home while he was out being him. I got dressed, stepped out, and sure enough… There he was. Out. Loud. Real loud.

And he wasn't just entertaining anyone—he was deep in it with *one of them.* The way she touched him, laughed too hard, leaned in too close… I knew.

So, I walked up. Calm. Controlled.

He denied everything, of course. But she? She had no filter. Dates, texts, late nights, she spilled it all. My calm flipped into chaos. We argued. He lied. She ran off. And there I stood—heart cracked wide open, clarity cutting sharper than any knife.

Then came the baby mama drama. And one thing about a man with unfinished business? It always comes back messy.

I tried for a few weeks to patch things up. We talked. We cried. We spun in circles. But the damage was done. I was exhausted. He couldn't keep his timelines straight, and I couldn't keep pretending.

Then the truth hit me like a final blow—the baby mama was pregnant. And not long after, the baby didn't make it. The loss was heavy, but in a strange way, it marked the end for me. Something in me broke and healed at the same time.

That chapter, with all its chaos, confusion, and heartbreak, closed itself. There were no more explanations to chase, no more apologies to wait on. Just silence. And in that silence, I finally found my answer, and it was time to let go.

We went our separate ways.

He tried to reel me back in with more trips, more promises, more illusions. But I was done. Tired of the mind games. Tired of losing myself in someone else's shadow.

That chapter of my life? Closed.

For the first time in a long time, I was finally free.

And for the first time in a long time, I remembered who I was outside of anyone else, outside of the chaos, outside of the glitter that had once blinded me.

I had stepped into my own power.

This time, I wasn't running from my past; I was walking toward my purpose.

Chapter 5:
The Sudden Shift

Proverbs 3:5–6 (NIV)
"Trust in the Lord with all your heart and lean not on
your own understanding; in all your ways submit to him,
and he will make your paths straight."

After the breakup, something inside me began to ache for peace—the kind of peace I had spent years running from. I wanted more than nights out, industry men, and surface-level thrills. I wanted healing. I wanted God.

Truth is, my relationship with God didn't start in that moment—it started years earlier. When I was younger, I'd spend time with my dad's mom, who was a pastor. She kept me active in church and singing in the choir, helping at events, and showing up for Sunday service no matter what. She didn't just talk about faith; she lived it. Even when I strayed, those seeds she planted never left me. They were buried deep, waiting for the right season to grow.

Similarly, when I spent time with my grandmother, my mom's mom, she kept me active in church through talent shows, singing in the choir, ushering, and other activities—anything that kept me from fading into the background.

So, when life fell apart, I didn't find God; I *remembered* Him. I went back to the foundation my grandmother had built in me, back to the prayers I didn't know were still covering me.

I started attending every service I could—Sunday mornings, midweek Bible studies, conferences, and prayer calls. You name it, I was there. Eventually, I began serving under a powerful woman of God, and in that season, I learned more about myself than I ever had in all my years of chasing the world. I was pouring myself into ministry, praying with purpose, and finally trusting God with everything—my heart, my healing, my future.

Falling in love wasn't on my radar anymore, not after the betrayal, the manipulation, the mind games. I was building my real estate business, reconnecting with old passions, and pursuing my massage therapy license—something I had put on the back burner for far too long.

But more than anything, I was rebuilding *myself.* The version of me that had been buried under disappointment, heartbreak, and compromise. I was learning to rest instead of rush, to pray instead of panic, to choose peace over proving a point.

There were nights I cried myself to sleep, not because I missed him, but because I was grieving the woman I used to be and the one who settled for half-love and called it enough. God was stripping away everything that wasn't meant for me, and though it hurt, it was holy work.

I started to see purpose in the pain. Every tear became a seed, every heartbreak a lesson. My confidence began to return—not the kind built on validation or attention, but the quiet kind that comes from knowing who you are in God.

For the first time in a long time, I wasn't chasing anything or anyone. I was becoming.

I wasn't rushing my process anymore. I let myself feel everything—the anger, the disappointment, the loneliness, and instead of running from it, I laid it at God's feet. I stopped trying to control outcomes and started learning the art of surrender.

There was a quiet strength growing inside me. The kind that doesn't need to announce itself. The kind that comes from surviving things that should've broken you. I learned to enjoy my own company again—coffee in the morning with worship music playing softly in the background, long drives with no destination, journaling my prayers until they turned into praise.

People around me started to notice the change. They'd say, "You look different," not realizing it wasn't the makeup or the clothes, but it was *peace*. I was finally at peace.

I began to forgive—not just him, but myself. For staying too long. For ignoring red flags. For thinking I had to be everything to someone who was never ready to be anything for me. That forgiveness was the final key that unlocked the version of me I had been waiting to meet.

Opportunities started to open up, and doors I didn't have to force. My business grew, my circle shifted, and my discernment sharpened. I learned to guard my spirit, to move in silence, and to let God handle what I couldn't.

This season wasn't about revenge or proving anyone wrong. It was about restoration, about learning that sometimes the blessing isn't in what you gain, but in what you finally let go of.

And as I stood in the middle of my healing, I realized that I had become the woman I used to pray to be. Whole. Grounded. At peace.

Through all of that, I remained focused on God and school. Becoming a Licensed Massage Therapist wasn't just a career move; it was a calling. Every class, every late-night study session, every test I passed felt like a step toward redemption. Massage therapy became more than just learning the body; it was about acknowledging the spirit, mind, and soul.

There were days when exhaustion crept in, when old wounds tried to reopen, when the enemy whispered that I wasn't strong enough to start over. But I kept pressing. I reminded myself that discipline was a form of worship, that consistency was its own kind of prayer.

As I balanced school, motherhood, and ministry, I began to see how everything I'd been through was getting me ready for this season. God was teaching me endurance, patience, and faith in motion. What once felt like loss was now shaping my purpose.

Each time I laid my hands to study, to work, or to pray, I felt His presence guiding me. He was guiding me that the same hands that once held pain were now being trained to bring healing.

Through it all, I stayed focused—on God, on school, on the woman I was becoming. I stopped chasing what had left me empty and started nurturing what filled me up. Every late night of studying, every quiet prayer whispered between tears, every small victory reminded me that I was exactly where I was supposed to be.

The journey wasn't easy, but it was holy. God was pruning, stretching, and molding me in ways I didn't always understand, yet deep down I knew it was all working together for my good.

When I finally earned my license, it wasn't just a career milestone; it was a symbol of *rebirth*. Proof that broken things can be rebuilt, that lost girls can find themselves again, and that nothing surrendered to God is ever wasted.

I didn't need closure from anyone. I didn't need apologies or explanations. I had peace. Real peace. The kind that doesn't depend on circumstances but flows from within, and peace that could only come from God.

That was the moment I knew the old chapter had closed for good. The heartbreak, the confusion, the searching, it all led me here.

To purpose.

To wholeness.

To freedom.

And as I stepped into this new season, I carried one truth with me:

I was no longer surviving,

I was *becoming her.*

Chapter 6:
When Stillness Spoke

Psalm 46:10
"Be still, and know that I am God."

That's when he came along.

He was nothing like what I was used to, no flashy chains, no street reputation. He was… regular. An Army vet. Kind of awkward. Quiet. Persistent. For weeks, he kept trying to talk to me. I kept brushing him off. I couldn't figure out why I resisted him so much, maybe because he felt too safe… too still. And I wasn't used to stillness.

Eventually, I gave in. I gave him my number. We talked. He seemed decent enough—attentive, engaging, said all the right things. He kept asking me to hang out, take a drive, go bowling, or go to dinner. I told him I lived an hour away. He didn't flinch. "I'll drive," he said.

I wasn't impressed. I wanted an excuse to push him away, but I couldn't find one that stuck. One slow afternoon, I finally texted him my address. When I opened the door and saw him standing there in floral shorts and a slightly faded tee, I just stared. This is who drove an hour for me? Looking like he just rolled off his couch?

But since he came all that way, I gave him a chance. We hit a few stores and grabbed some food. He had charm—a quiet charm, and he knew how to win someone over with words and attentiveness. Or at least he made it look that way.

From that day on, we were nearly inseparable. We dated for six months leading up to the proposal, and a year after we first met, we were married.

At first, I thought it was sweet. Maybe he was just into me. But as time passed, I started to wonder if it was really about love or if he was just running from something. He had a roommate. He didn't talk much about his past. And there were shadows behind his smile that I hadn't noticed before.

But he played the role well. He worshipped with me. Prayed with me. Talked about God like he knew Him. We'd lie in bed listening to worship music, and for a moment, I thought I had finally found a man who could match me spiritually.

After all the healing, the surrender, the focus on God made me believe maybe this was my reward. The good man I had been waiting for. The one that wouldn't break me.

Then came the proposal.

It wasn't elaborate or over-the-top, but it was sincere—or at least it felt that way. His words were tender. His promises sounded like redemption. I said yes because I wanted to believe that God could write a love story for me, too. I wanted to think that after all the pain, something beautiful could finally last.

His mom was all for it in the beginning and almost too involved. At times, it felt like I was competing with her for his attention. It was weird, but I brushed it off, thinking maybe it was just a close-knit bond.

Then came wedding week… and she vanished.

No calls. No texts. No explanation. His father didn't show up either. He was devastated, spent the morning of our wedding driving around the city in a panic, searching for something he never found, his parents' approval.

I was in the bridal suite, getting ready, surrounded by laughter, music, and my girls hyping me up. But inside, I felt the weight of something I couldn't explain. In the shower that morning, I cried so hard I thought my chest would cave in. I begged God for peace, for clarity. I didn't want to go through with it—but I felt trapped by the plans, the people, the moment.

When my father came to walk me down the aisle, I looked him dead in the eyes and whispered, "I can't do this."

He didn't understand. He thought it was nerves. Told me to breathe. Told me I could. But what he didn't realize was that it wasn't my flesh speaking, but it was my spirit.

Still, I walked down that aisle.

The wedding was stunning—outdoor, waterfront, my dad even sang before giving me away. The reception was magical. But none of it could silence the uneasiness sitting heavy in my soul.

That night, I expected to finally have a moment of peace. To start my life as a wife. Instead, I walked into chaos. The hotel room—our wedding night suite—was full of his cousins and groomsmen... frying chicken like it was a block party. I was disgusted. Exhausted.

When I questioned him, he looked at me like I was the problem.

That night was hell. Not love. Not joy. Not intimacy. Just tension, frustration, and the slow unraveling of everything I thought I had just committed to.

That night, I didn't sleep next to my husband.

I slept next to a stranger.

The shift had already begun.

The honeymoon phase was short-lived, as if it ever existed at all. The man who once couldn't go a day without checking in suddenly became distant. His tone changed. His eyes changed. His priorities changed. I started to feel like a burden instead of a blessing.

He didn't want to pray anymore. Didn't want to talk about God. The worship playlists were replaced with silence, tension, and unspoken resentment. His patience thinned, and mine was constantly tested. It was like living with two different men—the one I met and the one I married.

I tried to hold on. Tried to remember the sweet beginnings. Wanted to remind myself that marriage takes work. But it felt like I was the only one working. Every disagreement turned into blame. Every tear I cried was met with indifference. And slowly, I started shrinking.

He became colder with each passing day. Nights were long and quiet. Mornings felt heavy. I'd wake up before him just to pray, whispering to God for the strength I no longer had. I didn't recognize the woman staring back at me in the mirror anymore. She looked tired, dimmed, and drained of the light she fought so hard to find.

The man who once quoted Scripture began using it as a weapon, to guilt, to twist, to justify. And the woman who once stood boldly in her faith began questioning her own discernment. How could I have missed the signs? How could I, after everything I'd been through, still end up here?

There were moments when I'd walk into the massage studio, my sacred space, and feel my spirit come alive again. The peace I felt there reminded me that I hadn't lost God, even if I was losing my marriage. I'd breathe, pray, and ask Him to help me hold on just a little longer. But deep down, I knew that I was trying to resurrect something He never built.

It's a strange kind of grief, mourning a marriage that's still breathing. You wake up every day next to someone who's supposed to love you, but their presence feels like an absence. Their silence feels louder than their words.

I stopped trying to fix it. Stopped begging for communication or change. Stopped carrying a weight that was never mine to hold.

One night, I lay there in the dark, tears streaming quietly onto my pillow, and whispered, "God, if this isn't where I'm supposed to be… show me."

And He did. Not all at once, but piece by piece. Through hidden messages, lies that unraveled, and truths that could no longer stay buried. The man I thought was my safe place became my lesson.

That's when I realized, the enemy doesn't always come to destroy you through chaos. Sometimes, he sends comfort. A distraction dressed as stability. A counterfeit blessing that feels familiar enough to make you question your discernment.

And once again, I found myself standing in the middle of a storm I never saw coming. But this time, I wasn't the same woman I used to be. I didn't beg. I didn't break. I prayed. I waited. I watched.

Slowly, God started showing me who he really was… and reminding me who I still was.

And I began to see something clearly for the first time: I didn't need a man to complete me. I didn't need approval to validate myself. I didn't need someone else's love to confirm God's love for me.

This was the moment my power returned. Piece by piece, prayer by prayer, I reclaimed the woman I had fought so hard to become. I was no longer chasing a fairy tale or tolerating what wasn't meant for me.

I was stepping into freedom, clarity, and wholeness—and for the first time in my life, I knew: I would never again dim my light for anyone else.

Chapter 7:
Unexpected News

Romans 8:28
"And we know that in all things God works for the good of those who love him, who have been called according to his purpose."

Months after the wedding, I was just going through the motions. Smiling in public, crying in private. Living with a man I barely recognized, someone who had promised me forever but delivered confusion, isolation, and emotional chaos.

I tried to focus on work, tried to throw myself into real estate and massage school. I kept showing up, smiling, grinding... but something in me felt off. I wasn't just exhausted. I wasn't just emotional. I was different.

Then it hit me—my cycle was late.

At first, I brushed it off. Stress, maybe. My body had been through so much, especially mentally and emotionally. But something deeper whispered, *Check.* So, I did.

I stared at the test in silence, heart pounding louder than the second line that appeared before my eyes.

Pregnant.

I sat on the edge of the tub, hands shaking, mind racing, heart screaming. I was pregnant. Pregnant… by a man I had just married but didn't fully know. Pregnant in the middle of confusion, exhaustion, and spiritual warfare.

This wasn't the plan.

I wasn't one of those women who dreamed of building a family with a broken man, hoping he'd change because of a child. I had lived enough life to know that a baby doesn't fix what's fractured. It only magnifies it.

But here I was, carrying life. And that life was depending on me.

I didn't cry at first. I was too numb to cry. It was a mix of emotions, fear, shock, disbelief… and a tiny sliver of hope I was too afraid to admit. Maybe this would ground him. Perhaps this would settle the chaos. Maybe…

When I told him, his face said everything his mouth didn't.

He said the right things. Said he was happy. That we'd get through it together, but something in his eyes looked trapped, as if the weight of responsibility was already too much. I could see it. Feel it. And I hated that I could feel it.

Days passed. Weeks. His mood started to shift again. The drinking picked up. The arguments got heavier. The control got tighter. And there I was, pregnant, vulnerable, trying to survive an emotional hurricane with a fake smile and swollen ankles.

There were nights I'd sit in my car and cry. Not because I didn't want the baby, but because I didn't like the life, I saw unfolding around the baby.

I wrestled with guilt. With fear. With the memory of the girl I used to be—the fun girl, the wild girl, the dreamer. And now, here I was… again in a familiar place with a different man and a deeper ache.

I had to make decisions not just about the baby but for me as well.

I knew I couldn't let this child grow up in chaos. I knew I couldn't sacrifice myself at the altar of a relationship that was slowly draining the light out of me. I had already lost too much of myself trying to "make it work."

So, I started making moves—quietly, prayerfully.

Therapy. Support groups. Journaling. Prayer. Boundaries. I began reclaiming the parts of me I had given away, the parts that laughed freely, that dreamed boldly, that loved without compromise. I started planning for motherhood, but not as a wife, as a woman who refused to let another storm destroy her peace.

And then it hit me—the reality of starting over. My first born, my daughter was 20. Twenty years old. An adult in many ways, but still my baby. And here I was, stepping into motherhood again, this time with the wisdom I hadn't had the first time. I couldn't change the past, but I could do this right. I could show her love without compromise, without fear, without the chaos I had once tolerated.

And deep down, I started to remember the promise. That even in my mess, God was still writing my story. That maybe, just maybe, this child was a turning point, not a punishment.

I leaned into my faith harder than ever. I prayed for wisdom, for protection, for clarity. I asked God to teach me to be a mother who was strong, present, and unshakable. And in those prayers, I felt a peace I hadn't known in years—a whisper reminding me that life could still be beautiful, even when it looked messy.

This wasn't how I expected the next chapter of my life to begin.

But ready or not, it had already started.

And for the first time in a long time, I realized something: I wasn't just surviving this storm. I was preparing to rise from it. Stronger. Wiser. Whole.

I was starting over with motherhood, and this time, I knew who I was. I knew my worth. I knew my boundaries. And I knew that no matter what came next, God had already equipped me to handle it.

32

Chapter 8:
Alone, But Not Really

Pregnancy is supposed to be this beautiful, glowing time in a woman's life. People paint it like a Hallmark movie with maternity photos, baby showers, and late-night cravings with your partner running out to satisfy them.

But for me? It felt like I was holding my breath underwater, smiling through suffocation.

I wasn't technically alone, no, I had a husband. But emotionally, spiritually, mentally… I'd never felt more isolated in my life.

The man I married, the one who had once talked about building a future and being a family man, was unraveling before my eyes. And while he unraveled, I was growing life inside of me, trying to keep it all together.

We didn't talk anymore. We argued. Or worse, sat in silence. The kind of silence that echoed louder than any fight. He was either distant or defensive. Drinking became his comfort. I became his target.

He'd accuse me of things that didn't make sense—jealous of my freedom when I had none. I was too tired to fight back, too pregnant to care. Most nights, I'd cry quietly, clutching my belly, whispering to my unborn child, "I got you. Even if no one else does, I've got you."

I didn't tell many people what was going on. I didn't want the "I told you so's," or the pity, or the judgment. I had worn a mask for so long, I didn't even know how to take it off anymore. People saw the strong woman, the ambitious girl from the city who always bounced back. But inside? I was breaking.

The only place I found peace was in God. My prayer became my life, my therapy. Some nights I'd be up, pacing the floors, talking to Him like He was sitting across from me.

"God, what is this? Why would you bring me here? I thought I was doing better. I thought I was healing."

And the answer didn't come in a loud, booming voice. It came in stillness. In moments where I should've lost my mind but didn't. In the strength I didn't know I had.

I started talking to my baby more. I would lay my hands on my belly and speak life:

"You're not a mistake. You're not a trap. You're not a burden. You are mine, and I'm going to do everything in my power to make sure you never feel what I'm feeling right now."

I didn't know how I was going to do it. I didn't have all the answers. But I had made up my mind. This child would not be raised in dysfunction. I would not repeat the cycles I swore to break. I'd rather be alone and at tranquility than connected and in chaos.

I nursed hope along with my unborn child. I pictured the home I would create for them, the love I would give unconditionally, the stability I would protect fiercely. Even in the middle of chaos, I promised them safety, comfort, and unwavering devotion.

Pregnancy has a way of exposing everything from love, fear, weakness, to truth. It strips away the filters and forces you to see people for who they really are.

As my belly grew, so did the distance between us. He became colder, sharper with his words. I tried to keep the environment calm, to make the home feel safe, to keep myself from stressing, as it wasn't good for the baby. But I was living in a house that felt like a battlefield and walking on eggshells while trying to grow life inside me.

He would still go to my appointments. And we would sit beside each other like strangers. I'd sit in waiting rooms feeling alone, hands resting on my stomach, pretending not to notice the couples holding hands beside me. The nurses would ask, "How are you feeling today?" and I'd just smile politely, knowing my silence said everything.

At night, I'd pray over my stomach. I'd whisper to the baby, "It's me and you, okay? We're going to be fine." I didn't know how, but I believed it. I had to.

There were days my faith carried me when my body felt too heavy to move. I remember massaging my swollen feet after long shifts, whispering scriptures just to keep myself from breaking down. Every kick reminded me that something good was still growing, even in the middle of chaos.

Meanwhile, his behavior grew more unpredictable. The drinking got worse. The arguments turned cruel. He'd disappear for hours, sometimes overnight, and when I questioned him, I'd be met with deflection, gaslighting, or silence.

The emotional distance became a canyon I couldn't cross. I stopped expecting softness. I stopped hoping for a connection. I just focused on survival.

And yet, somehow, amidst the hurt, God gave me the calmness I asked for. A quiet kind, the kind that doesn't erase the pain but helps you stand in the middle of it without losing your mind.

One night, after another explosive argument, I sat in the car parked outside our house, hands trembling on the steering wheel, and I made a decision.

I couldn't keep choosing someone who kept choosing to hurt me.

That night, I stopped begging. I stopped explaining. I stopped shrinking myself to be palatable for a man who didn't even like the healed version of me.

I went inside, laid my hand on my stomach, and prayed a simple prayer:

"Lord, protect this child. Protect my mind. And if this isn't love, remove me before it kills me."

That prayer became my turning point.

From that night on, I began preparing not just for the baby's arrival, but for whatever was to come. Quietly. Strategically. Spiritually.

I built a new kind of faith, one rooted in reality, not potential.

The pregnancy was hard. Lonely. But sacred. Because through every tear, every sleepless night, every whispered prayer, I realized that God wasn't just growing a child inside me—He was growing me.

By the time my due date approached, I was no longer the same woman who had stood at that altar. I wasn't desperate for love. I was desperate for peace.

And I knew deep down that when the baby came, so would my courage.

Chapter 9:
New Life, New Role

2 Corinthians 5:17
"Therefore, if anyone is in Christ, the new creation has
come: The old has gone, the new is here!"

The day had finally come.

After months of emotional warfare, swollen feet, sleepless nights, and whispering promises to my unborn child, I was about to bring life into the world yet again. You would think the moment would be sacred, powerful, full of tears, prayers, and gratitude. And it was… but not in the way I imagined.

Because while I was bringing new life into the world, I was also watching the last pieces of the old version of me fall away.

Labor started slowly but intensely. My body was working. My soul was praying. Nurses were in and out. Machines beeping. Fluorescent lights. Pain and pressure and moments of fear. And then he was in the room, pacing like he was the one in labor.

He was there… but I wish he hadn't been.

From the moment we walked into the hospital, he made it about him—his nerves, his comfort, his image. He did rub my back and sometimes hold my hand. The only words of strength he offered were, "You got this." But even those words felt hollow, drowned out by his constant calls, his complaints about tiredness, about how seeing me in pain affected him.

I remember gripping the side of the bed, body on fire, breath ragged, and glancing at him slouched in the corner chair, scrolling through his phone like he was waiting for an Uber, not witnessing the miracle unfolding. I thought, He doesn't get it. He'll never get it.

When it was time to push, I reached deep inside myself, not just physically, but spiritually. I went into battle. Every breath, every contraction, every scream carried the weight of every lie, every heartbreak, every disappointment, every time I had been asked to carry more than I was built for.

And when that baby cried, something inside of me was reborn.

They handed me my child, and looking at this perfect little being, wide-eyed and full of innocence, and in that moment, I knew:

This is the love I've been searching for. This is what real, pure, unconditional love feels like.

I nursed my baby, feeling the intimacy of connection grow with every feed. Every latch was a reminder that I could nurture life even in the midst of chaos. That I could give fully, even when my own heart felt fractured.

I looked at my baby and made a vow:

You will never feel unloved. You will never feel alone. You will never have to question your worth because I will spend the rest of my life showing you just how valuable you are.

Meanwhile, he was asking for someone to take a picture of him holding the baby, as if he had done the hard part. Posting it online. Captioning it like he was the hero of the story.

"Proud dad moment."

He smiled for the camera, while I bled in silence.

The postpartum room was cold, not just from the air, but from the space between us. He slept like a rock while I was up every two hours, feeding, burping, changing, healing, and adjusting. Alone in a room full of machines, and the man I once believed was my partner.

And yet, through the ache and exhaustion, there was joy.

Not because of him, but in spite of him.

Motherhood awakened something in me that no man ever could. It wasn't just about becoming a mom all over again, but it was about reclaiming my voice, my power, and my purpose.

I had brought life into the world. And with that same strength… I would learn to rebuild mine.

I began to see clearly that love doesn't require validation from anyone else. It doesn't ask permission or demand recognition. It lives in the small moments in the midnight feeds, the quiet cuddles, the first coos, the tiny hands that wrap around your finger and never let go.

And in those moments, I realized: I was enough. I always had been. The world could fall apart, people could fail me, but this little life depended on me, and I would rise to meet it.

It was in that sacred exhaustion, in that raw, unfiltered space, that I understood a truth I had been running toward my entire life: the strongest love isn't romantic. It isn't conditional. It isn't performative. The strongest love is the one you cultivate in your own heart and pour into those who depend on you, unshakable, unwavering, and unstoppable.

That day, I became the woman who would never settle for less than she deserved. The woman who would never dim her light to make someone else comfortable. The woman who would carry her child and herself into a life she would design and protect with fierce love.

Life had tested me, beaten me, and tried to break me. But in this hospital room, as I held my child for the very first time, I understood: some things were meant to be born from pain. And I was ready to rise.

Pregnancy had stripped everything away: pretense, pride, control, and left me with only what mattered: God, my children, and myself. Every late-night prayer, every whispered word to my belly, every tear I cried alone in the dark became part of a preparation not just for my baby's life, but for my own.

I learned to trust my instincts. To speak life. To nurture hope when the world around me felt heavy and hostile. I vowed to myself this child would know safety, love, and calmness, things I hadn't always been afforded. I nursed not only my baby but my spirit, reminding myself I could give everything even when I had been given so little.

By the time I walked into the hospital, I was no longer just the young woman trying to survive marriage, abuse, and betrayal. I was a mother, a protector, a warrior carrying more than just life; I carried my purpose.

Labor wasn't long. It was exhausting, and minor pain consumed me. And yet, every scream, every contraction, every push felt like shedding another layer of the past. With every breath, I reclaimed pieces of myself that had been hidden under chaos. When my baby cried for the first time, the sound didn't just fill the room; it filled me with the truth I had been running toward my entire life: love begins with me, and I am enough.

The man I married was there, but he could not touch the power of that moment. He was absent in the ways that mattered most. His presence was hollow, but it could not steal my triumph. I nursed my baby, and as life flowed from me to them, I felt an unshakable certainty: I could survive anything. I could rise from anything.

Motherhood had awakened a fierceness I didn't know I possessed. This wasn't just a child's birth; it was my rebirth. And I carried that truth with me into every late-night feed, every quiet prayer, every tear shed in the dark.

Chapter 10:
Grief, Growth, and Grit

James 1:2-4
"Consider it pure joy, my brothers and sisters, whenever
you face trials of many kinds, because you know the
testing of your faith produces perseverance. Let
perseverance finish its work so that you may be mature
and complete, not lacking anything."

No one tells you that grieving a relationship can feel just like grieving a death. And in some ways, it is.

You're mourning the version of them you believed in.

You're mourning the version of yourself that loved them.

You're mourning the dreams, the plans, the "someday" that never got the chance to live.

After giving birth, I didn't just leave the hospital with a baby in my arms; I left with the silent weight of disappointment on my chest. I had officially stepped into a new life while dragging the corpse of a dead relationship behind me.

There were days I missed him. Not because I wanted him back, but because I missed what I thought we were building. I wanted a family and not just a baby. I wanted a partnership, not just presence. But you can't build a home on broken promises and borrowed personalities. Deep down, I knew… he was never going to be the man I needed.

Still, the grief came in waves.

I cried while cleaning.
I cried, folding tiny clothes.

I cried while scrolling through my phone, deleting old pictures, blocking familiar numbers, and watching the lies he would post on social media go up while my trust in people went down.

And yet, in the midst of grief, I found growth. The silence became a sanctuary. The chaos I had once called "love" began to look like a prison. I started seeing things and people with new eyes. I saw who had truly been there and who had only come around for the highlight reel. That list got really short, really fast.

Single motherhood was not easy, but it sharpened me. It taught me how to stretch a dollar and my patience. It taught me how to show up even when I was tired, how to comfort a crying baby while holding in my own tears, how to run a business on two hours of sleep and a whole lot of prayer.

I nursed my son with intention, each feed a reminder of my strength and presence. I wasn't just nourishing a child, but I was reaffirming my power to protect, to love, and to create a safe world for someone who depended entirely on me. Every latch, every midnight cuddle, every soft whisper into his ear reminded me that life could still be tender and sacred, even in the midst of chaos.

I began leaning into God in ways I hadn't before. My prayers were no longer just words; they were lifelines. Every whispered "Thank You," and every desperate plea for guidance reminded me that I wasn't alone, that my children weren't alone, and that I didn't have to carry the weight of the world by myself.

I stopped waiting for an apology I was never going to get.

Stopped hoping for accountability from someone who couldn't even be honest with himself.

I stopped replaying the moments that broke me and started creating moments that built me.

My children became my compass, my reason, my reset. In the quiet hours, while the baby napped and the world kept spinning, I sat with myself. I read. I wrote. I prayed. I healed. I reflected on the young girl I once was, the one chasing nightlife, validation, and chaos, and I recognized her courage, too. She had survived. She had learned. And now, she was guiding me into this new season.

There was grit in my grind now. A fire that came from knowing I survived it all. And not only did I survive… I still loved. I still laughed. I still dreamed.

I discovered that strength isn't just physical endurance. It's the quiet, consistent choices you make every day to rise above what tries to break you. It's in showing up when you feel broken. It's in giving love even when the world feels cold. It's in holding your child and whispering, "We're going to be okay," even when your own heart is raw and fragile.

Because the biggest plot twist wasn't the heartbreak, or the betrayal, or the loneliness.

It was that after everything, I still chose myself.

I chose peace.

I chose purpose.

I chose to be the woman I needed when I was hurting.

And I began to see that healing doesn't happen overnight. It's quiet. It's relentless. It's messy and beautiful all at once. And through it, I realized I had been preparing for this moment my whole life, and the moment I would finally be enough for myself, and enough for my children, without needing anyone else's approval.

This was not the life I planned. But it was becoming the life I owned.

Every day, I learned more about who I was outside of anyone else's shadow. Every prayer, every tear, every hug with my children reinforced that I had the power to rebuild, to nurture, to protect, and to thrive. My story was no longer about surviving a relationship that failed me, but it was about creating a legacy of love, resilience, and faith.

I wasn't just a mother, a daughter, or a woman who had been hurt— I was a force. A woman who had walked through fire and came out glowing, a woman who had faced loss and heartbreak and found purpose in it. A woman who knew that no matter what, God had always been faithful, even when people were not.

And as I held my children close, whispered scriptures over their little lives, and felt their tiny hands wrap around my fingers, I understood: I had finally come home, to my heart, to my purpose, and to my calling.

Because some chapters don't end with closure like others, they end with peace. They end with acknowledging your worth. They end with the quiet, unshakable certainty that you are exactly where you're supposed to be.

And for me, that chapter was mine. Fully, unapologetically, and beautifully mine.

Chapter 11:
Becoming Her

There comes a moment when you stop looking back and start standing up.

Not because everything is fixed. Not because you suddenly "got over it."

But because something inside of you whispers…

"You deserve more."

That whisper turned into a roar for me.

I had spent so long a day surviving and pushing through heartbreak, carrying the weight of motherhood, running on fumes and faith. But I was done just surviving. It was time to start living, and this time for real for me.

I looked in the mirror one day and realized I no longer recognized the woman staring back, not in a sad way… in a powerful way. She wasn't the broken girl begging to be loved anymore. She wasn't the people-pleaser, the "ride-or-die," the woman shrinking herself to fit into a version of life she never asked for.

She was becoming her.

Wiser. Softer. Stronger.

A woman born from fire, but glowing like grace.

I started redefining what success meant for me.

It wasn't just closing real estate deals or posting cute pictures.

It was peace of mind.

It was protecting my space.

It was choosing what felt good over what just looked good.

It was knowing that I didn't have to prove my worth to anyone because my worth was already written in God's blueprint before I ever made a mistake.

The healing didn't happen all at once.

Some days, I felt fierce. Other days, I felt fragile.

But even in my fragility, I was free.

I started doing things that made me smile, things like journaling, traveling, taking myself out, pouring into my daughter with love that overflowed from a healing heart. I began dreaming again, and not the kind of dreams that depend on someone else's potential, but dreams rooted in my purpose. I stopped asking, *"Why me?"* and started saying, *"Watch me."*

Watch me rebuild.

Watch me reclaim.

Watch me rise.

I created new boundaries. I said "no" more than I used to, and didn't feel guilty about it.

I forgave myself for what I didn't know then, and gave myself credit for having the courage to leave, heal, and grow.

And eventually, the things I used to beg for?

Love. Calmness. Respect. Support.

They started flowing into my life and not from desperation, but from alignment.

Because the moment I stopped chasing what wasn't meant for me...
Everything that was started finding me.

So yes, I grieved.

Yes, I stumbled.

Yes, I cried in silence when no one saw me holding it all together.

But more than that, I rose.

I bloomed.

And I became the woman I used to pray for.

Motherhood taught me strength I never knew I had. Nursing my son, soothing him through midnight cries, and loving my daughter with a tenderness born of healing reminded me daily that life could still be beautiful. They were my compass, my heartbeat, my reminder that everything I had endured was not in vain.

This chapter isn't just the end of survival.

It's the beginning of sovereignty.

Of walking in power. Of choosing joy. Of becoming her.

The healed version.

The whole version.

The unstoppable version.

I learned that my worth is not defined by the love I receive, the approval I earn, or the mistakes I make. My worth is intrinsic, unshakable, and eternal.

I learned that peace is not the absence of pain, but it is the courage to stand in the storm and refuse to be broken.

I learned that happiness is not a gift others give; it is a decision I make every single day.

And I learned that when you finally stop chasing what isn't yours to hold, God rearranges your life, filling the spaces with purpose, clarity, and the kind of love that aligns with your soul.

I am no longer surviving.

I am living.

I am free.

I am whole.

I am her.

And this is only the beginning!

Chapter 12:
A letter to my Mom

Ephesians 4:32
"Be kind and compassionate to one another, forgiving each other, just as in Christ God forgave you."

Mom,

I need to tell you things I never said out loud. Things I carried in silence for years. Things that left wounds I didn't know how to name.

There were moments in my life when I felt abandoned by you. Times I needed you, your guidance, your presence, and I felt like you weren't there. I carried that hurt with me through the nights I cried alone, the prayers I whispered for your attention and love. I needed my mom, and I felt unseen.

And I know now that life isn't simple. I know you had your battles, your burdens, your responsibilities. I know you loved me in your way, even when it didn't feel like enough. But I need you to know how it felt from my side that the ache of longing, the questions, the small disappointments stacked into years.

Mom, I forgive you. I forgive you for the times I felt small, for the times I wished you were different, for the times I resented what I thought I didn't have. Forgiveness isn't forgetting, and it's not pretending the hurt didn't exist, but it's me releasing it so it no longer controls me.

I forgive myself too—for holding onto anger too long, for blaming you for things that were never entirely yours to fix, for expecting perfection from a human heart.

Even in the hurt, I see the love you gave, the lessons, the faith, the strength you passed down, whether I acknowledged them then or not. And I see the ways you've tried, even when life made it messy.

Mom, I want us to heal. I want to rewrite the story of our relationship and not erase the past, but to honor it and move forward with grace. I want to build a bond that isn't defined by absence or disappointment, but by understanding, compassion, and love.

Thank you for being my mom, even when motherhood was complicated, even when life made it hard to show up the way we both needed. Thank you for the faith you instilled in me, the foundation that kept me standing even when I felt alone.

I am letting go of the weight of resentment, the longing for what could have been, and the pain of feeling unseen. I am choosing forgiveness. I am choosing peace. I am choosing you, Mom, flawed, human, and still my mother.

With love and understanding,
Samone'

Chapter 13:
A letter to my Dad

Psalm 68:5
"A father to the fatherless, a defender of widows, is God in his holy dwelling"

Dad,

I have so much I need to say to you, things I've held inside for years, emotions I didn't know how to voice without feeling guilty or ashamed.

There were moments I felt abandoned by you. Times I needed your guidance, your protection, your presence, and it wasn't there. I wanted your approval, your encouragement, your simple acknowledgment that I mattered. But instead, I often felt like I was navigating life alone, carrying burdens I didn't fully understand.

I remember wishing you'd see me, hear me, understand me. I remember longing for a father's reassurance, a hand to hold, a voice to remind me that no matter what, I was enough. And when that didn't come, it left holes in my heart that I tried to fill with people, places, and distractions that never satisfied.

Dad, I forgive you. I forgive you for the ways I felt unseen, unheard, or unsupported. I forgive the absences, the missed moments, the mistakes, and because I know you did what you could with what you had. And I forgive myself for the resentment I carried for so long, for the anger I didn't know how to release, and for holding onto expectations that may have been impossible to meet.

Even in the pain, I recognize the lessons you passed down: the work ethic, the resilience, the drive to keep going even when life got hard. I carry those lessons with me, and I see now that they were your love showing up in the only way it knew how.

Dad, I want us to acknowledge the past without letting it define our future. I want to continue to build a relationship that isn't weighed down by guilt, regret, or distance but one grounded in understanding, respect, and love.

I am letting go of the feelings of abandonment, of longing for a version of fatherhood that didn't exist, and of the silence that once felt heavy in my chest. I am choosing forgiveness. I am choosing peace. I am choosing you, Dad—not perfection, not the father I imagined, but the man who gave me life and lessons in his own way.

With love and hope,
Samone'

Chapter 14:
A letter to my daughter

Jeremiah 29:11
"For I know the plans I have for you... Plans to prosper
you and not to harm you, plans to give you hope and a
future."

My baby girl Ja'Nyia,

If you're reading this one day, it means I found the strength to write through the tears, the joy, the scars, and the triumphs, all for you. Everything I've been through, everything I've endured, every mountain I've had to climb, it was never just about me. It was always, always for *you.*

You see, I wasn't always the woman I am today.

I had to grow through what I went through.

I had to fall and get back up.

I had to cry and still show up.

I had to be broken and still hold you in love.

But look at us now.

We're *still standing.*

I need you to know that life won't always be easy, baby girl.

It will test you. It will stretch you.

People will try to break you some out of ignorance, some out of pain, and some because they simply don't know what to do with a powerful woman wrapped in grace.

But I want you to remember this:

You come from strength.

You come from prayer.

You come from a woman who turned hardship into purpose.

There were days I wasn't sure we'd make it, especially when love felt like war, and peace felt like a luxury I couldn't afford.

But I kept going. For you. For us.

And through every sleepless night, every silent cry, every hard "no" I had to say, I found a deeper yes.

A yes to healing.

A yes to choosing me.

A yes to building a legacy you can be proud of.

You've seen me struggle, but I hope you also see me shine.

I hope you see how I rebuilt my life with cracked hands and a hopeful heart.

I hope you see how I learned to forgive not just others, but myself.

I hope you see how I never stopped dreaming, even when life tried to turn my dreams into dust.

I pray you learn to love yourself early.

I pray you protect your peace fiercely.

I pray you never shrink to make others comfortable.

And if you ever feel lost, I want you to close your eyes and remember who raised you.

You are not alone.

You are not too much.

You are not broken.

You are *becoming.*

And as long as I have breath, I'll be in your corner always whispering prayers, cheering from the front row, and reminding you that everything you need is already inside you.

So, walk boldly. Love deeply. Dream wildly.

And never forget where you come from.

A woman who was once buried by pain… but chose to bloom anyway.

With all the love in my soul,

Mommy

Chapter 15:
For My Sons

Psalm 127:3-4
"Sons are a heritage from the Lord, children a reward from
him. Like arrows in the hands of a warrior are sons born
in one's youth."

My Boys Genesis and Greyson,

You came into my life and changed everything.

Not because I wasn't already strong, but because loving you gave my strength direction.

Because of you, I fight harder. I pray deeper. And I love better.

You are gifts from God, living, breathing proof that light can rise from dark places and that purpose can be born out of pain.

I need you to know something from the very beginning:

Your worth has never depended on what you do, how tough you are, or who approves of you.

Your value was written on your soul the moment God formed you in my womb.

You are *loved.*

You are *needed.*

You are *chosen.*

Being your mother has stretched me in ways I never expected. It forced me to face the truth about broken love, emotional chaos, and the ache of raising you without the family I once imagined.

But through it all, you became my reason to rise.

And while your father's presence may have brought more storms than sunshine, I need you to understand this clearly:

You are not his mistakes.

You are not his limitations.

You are not the pain he never healed from.

You are your own men. And I will raise you to know the difference between *repeating cycles* and *breaking them.*

I will teach you to feel deeply.

To speak with love and lead with humility.

To own your mistakes, but never let them own you.

To understand that real strength isn't in how loud you yell or how hard you fight:

But in how gently you can love, how deeply you can think, and how boldly you can stand for what's right.

This world will try to harden you too soon.

It will tell you that men don't cry, that softness is weakness, that power means control.

But hear me when I say this:

There is nothing soft about being a man who heals.

There is nothing weak about choosing peace over ego.

And there is everything powerful about leading with love, intention, and integrity.

I pray you grow into men who know how to listen and not just to words, but to the silence between them.

Men who protect, not manipulate.

Who uplifts, not belittles.

Men who love with truth, respect, and friendship, not games, pride, or pain disguised as passion.

But most of all, I pray you never forget this:

You come from a woman who refused to let her pain parent her children.

A woman who didn't just survive —she *transformed.*

Every step I took to heal was so you wouldn't have to heal from me.

So, take up space, my sons.

Make your mark. Speak with your chest, but lead with your heart.

And know that no matter how tall you grow, how far you go, or how hard life gets,

You will always be the reason I kept going.

With every ounce of love I have,

Mommy 🩶

Chapter 16:
The Release (A letter to my husband)

Ephesians 4:31-32
"Get rid of all bitterness, rage, and anger...forgiving each other, just as in Christ God forgave you."

Husband,

This isn't a goodbye letter.

It's not about endings, it's about release. About peace. About growth.

For a long time, I carried the weight of what I thought we would be — the dreams we built, the plans we made, and the version of "us" I held on to even when it started to fade. I held on so tightly to what *was supposed to be* that I almost missed what *is*.

Our love story has seen the highest highs and the lowest lows. There were moments that felt like forever and others that made forever feel impossible. But through it all, one truth remains: I loved you, deeply, honestly, imperfectly. And somewhere in that love, I also learned the power of letting go... not of you, but of what I expected this to look like.

I forgive you, for the things you said, for the things you didn't say, and for the moments I felt unseen.

And I forgive myself for staying silent when I should've spoken, for carrying pain that wasn't mine to hold, for trying to fix what only God could heal.

Forgiveness doesn't mean I'm blind to what broke me. It just means I'm no longer allowing it to define how I love you or how I love myself.

I'm releasing the version of us that lived in my head, the one untouched by real life, untouched by struggle, untouched by growth. I'm choosing to see you as you are now: human, flawed, still learning, still evolving… just like me.

I don't know what our future looks like, and maybe that's okay. What I do know is that I no longer need to control the outcome to trust the process.

If we rebuild, I want it to be from a place of truth, not habit, not fear, not guilt, but *grace*.

And if we simply learn to love each other differently, then may that too be sacred.

I still believe in you, not just as my husband, but as a man becoming who God created you to be. I want you to grow, to heal, to rise. To confront the pain, you've buried and walk boldly in your purpose. Because your healing matters to me, even when we're not in perfect harmony.

Our story isn't over. It's just shifting. And maybe this chapter isn't about closure, maybe it's about clarity.

Maybe it's about learning that love isn't always loud or certain. Sometimes it's quiet. Sometimes it's patient. Sometimes it's two people finding their way back to themselves before they can truly find their way back to each other.

So, I release what I thought would be the picture-perfect version that never existed.

And I open my heart to what it *still can be.*

No bitterness. No blame. Just peace.

Because real love doesn't always look like fairy tales, sometimes it looks like forgiveness, reflection, and the courage to keep growing… together or apart.

With love,
Samone'

Chapter 17:
The Pen Belongs to God!

Psalm 138:8
"The Lord will perfect that which concerns me."

There was a time when I thought I knew exactly how my story would go, who would stay, who would love me right, and how the chapters would unfold.

I had a picture in my mind of how my life *should* have looked:

the perfect childhood, marriage, the steady happiness, the dream fulfilled without the detour of pain.

But life… life had other plans.

Some chapters broke me.

Others rebuilt me.

Some were written in tears.

Others in triumph.

And through it all, I kept trying to hold the pen,

To write the story *my* way.

Until I realized I was never the Author to begin with.

Every detour, every heartbreak, every blessing disguised as loss,

It all led me back to the same truth:

God has been writing this story all along.

The book I thought I didn't get to write?

It's being written every day,

through my healing, my motherhood, my faith, my growth.

Through the moments I wanted to give up, but didn't.

Through the times I questioned His timing, only to find out it was perfect all along.

I am not the author of a failed story.

I am the co-creator of a divine one,

still unfolding, still becoming, still guided by grace.

And the beauty of it all is this:

Even when I stop writing, **God keeps the story going.**

He edits what I thought was ruined.

He redeems what I thought was lost.

He writes endings that lead to beginnings, and beginnings that heal what once felt broken beyond repair.

So no,

I didn't get to write the book the way I imagined.

But maybe that was the point.

Because the Author,

the *real* Author,

had a better ending in mind.

And if there's one thing I know for sure…

He always has the final say.